the Big book of everything for boys

Chez Picthall & Christiane Gunzi

Contents

Created & produced by:
Picthall & Gunzi Limited
21A Widmore Road
Bromley
BR1 1RW
United Kingdom

Copyright © 2010
Picthall & Gunzi Limited

Original concept: Chez Picthall
Editorial: Christiane Gunzi and Katy Rayner
Design: Paul Calver
Education consultants: Diana Bentley, MA Advanced Dip. in Children's Literature, & Jane Whitwell, Diploma in Special Educational Needs

ISBN **978-1-906572-87-7**

Printed & bound in China

Picture credits: Andy Crawford; Argos; Ariel Skelley/CORBIS; Bernd Kohlhas/Corbis; Chez Picthall; Dietrich Rose/Corbis; FLPA; Giant - giant-bicycles.co.uk; istockphoto; John Lewis; Lakeland; Little Tikes; New Holland Agriculture; Photodisc; Steve Gorton; SW Productions/Brand X/Corbis; Tyler Shaw; Warren Photographic

Please note that every effort has been made to check the accuracy of the information contained in this book, and to credit the copyright holders correctly. Picthall & Gunzi apologise for any unintentional errors or omissions, and would be happy to include revisions to content and/or acknowledgments in subsequent editions of this book.

Full of fun brilliantly blue, *The Big Book of Everything for Boys* is a unique early-learning book created to entertain little boys everywhere. Using familiar themes, such as favorite foods and playtime, *The Big Book of Everything for Boys* covers the key concepts of counting, matching, patterns, opposites, colors and shapes. It also helps in building essential number and word recognition skills in preparation for the classroom.

Early reading skills are also encouraged, with the help of key vocabulary, word banks, finger tracing and maze games. By focusing on learning through play, *The Big Book of Everything for Boys* helps to build communication, comprehension and cognitive skills, and gives young readers confidence as they prepare for and start their important first years at school.

Bright, colorful photographs of familiar objects engage the child's interest.

Challenging interactive questions at the top of each page encourage communication and reading skills.

It's party time!
How many boys are at the birthday party?

balloons · party hats · sweets · party blowers · cakes

Are there more presents than children?
Are there enough biscuits for everyone?
Can every little boy have a party hat?

masks · biscuits · milkshake · lollipops · presents

Being busy at work
Count the chalks and find the matching number!

one notebook · two pairs of scissors · three pencil cases · four envelopes · five pencils · six chalks

1 2 3 4 5 6 7 8 9 10

Count the pencils and find the matching number!
How many paper clips can you count?
Let's count from one to ten!

seven gel pens · eight pieces of paper · nine erasers · ten paper clips

Stimulating, entertaining activities throughout the book encourage children to read and count.

Tiny soccer balls corresponding with every page number give boys something fun to find and count.

How to use this book

Planned with education experts and parents, *The Big Book of Everything for Boys* has been devised for adults and children to dip into together, and for children to enjoy on their own. The questions at the top of each page can be used as a starting point to help you get the most out of the book when time is precious. Every page also includes some kind of activity (*see* Contents page for details). By encouraging children to have fun with numbers and words, you will build their confidence and help them to enjoy reading and math when they start school. As you read the book together, invite your child to look beyond the pages too, and talk about the numbers, patterns, shapes and colors that you encounter in everyday life.

Above all, have fun!

Tips for reading this book

- Make sure that you and your child are comfortable before you start to look at the book.
- Work at your child's pace and allow him to choose some of the pages to look at when you begin reading.
- Give plenty of praise and encouragement, and always try to finish looking at the book on a positive note.
- Talk about, and look at any numbers and words that are special to your child.
- Point out numbers, pairs and groups of things when you are out and about together.
- Introduce your child to some fun activities, such as baking, which involve counting or weighing things.
- If you know any counting rhymes, why not teach them to your child?

My blue alphabet

How many letters are in the alphabet?

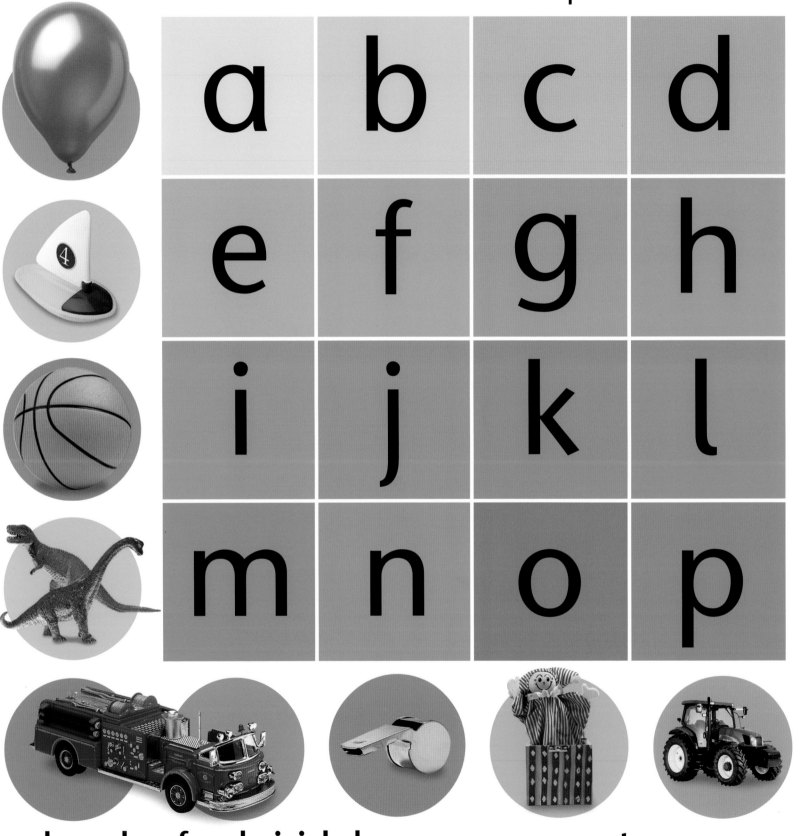

a b c d e f g h i j k l m n o p q r s t u v w x y z

Let's say the letters from **a** to **z**!

Point to the letter **b** for boy!

Which of the letters spell your name?

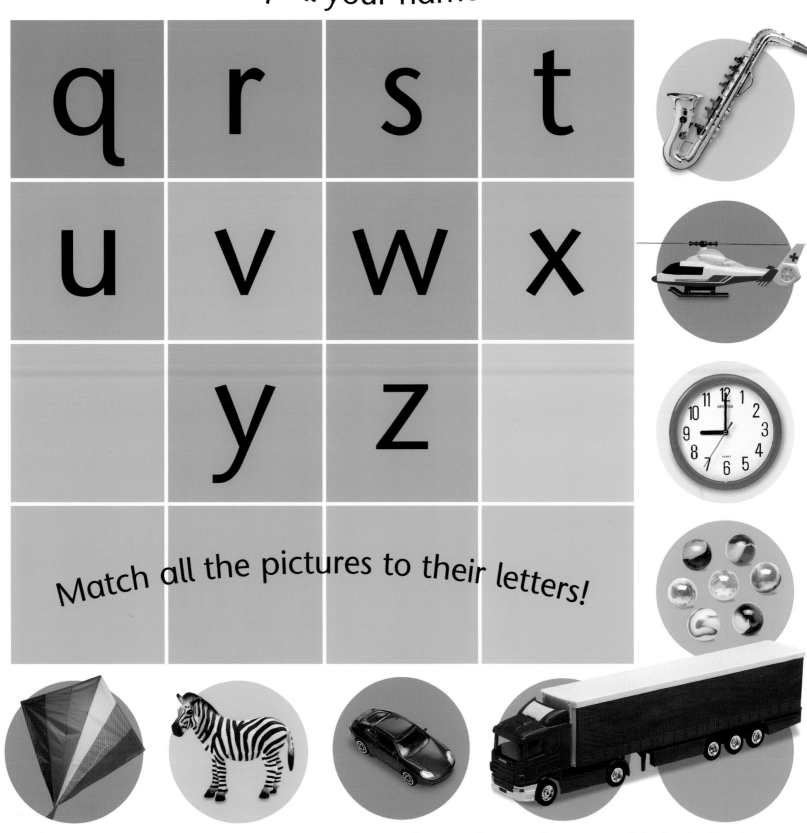

q	r	s	t
u	v	w	x
y	z		

Match all the pictures to their letters!

A B C D E F G H I J K L M N O P Q R S T U V W X Y Z

Being busy at work

Count the chalks and find the matching number!

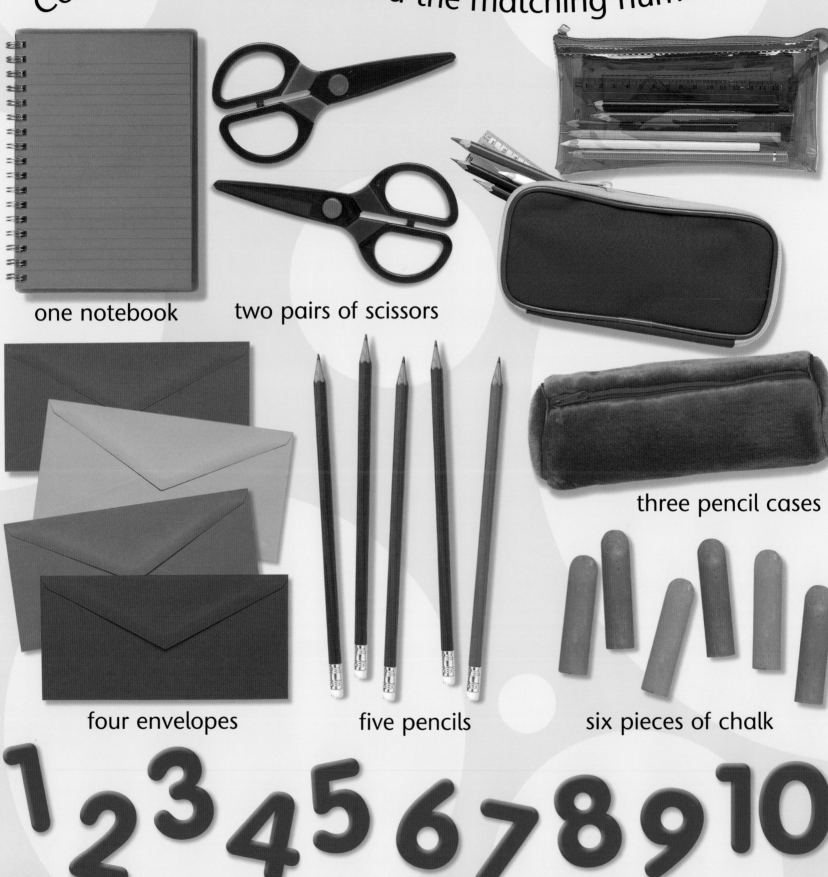

one notebook

two pairs of scissors

three pencil cases

four envelopes

five pencils

six pieces of chalk

1 2 3 4 5 6 7 8 9 10

Count the pencils and find the matching number!
How many paper clips can you count?
Let's count from one to ten!

seven gel pens

eight pieces
of paper

ten paper clips

nine erasers

My favorite things

Find the numbers from eleven to twenty!

eleven balls

twelve toy trucks

thirteen keyrings

fourteen marbles

fifteen toy animals

11 12 13 14 15

Count the marbles and find the matching number!
Point to the toy cars and find the number!
How many chocolates are there?

sixteen toy cars

seventeen candies

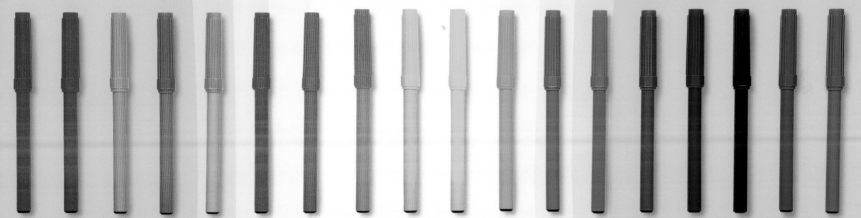

eighteen felt-tip pens

nineteen chocolates

twenty coloring pencils

16 17 18 19 20

Let's have a picnic!

Can you name all the picnic food?

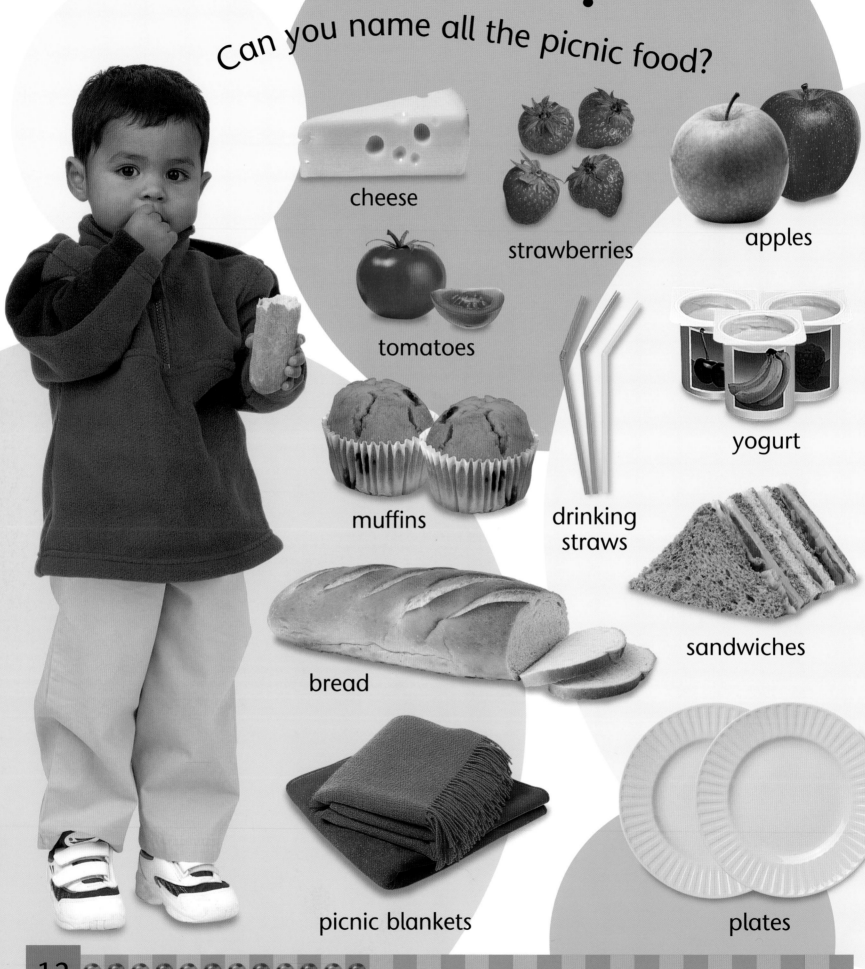

cheese

strawberries

apples

tomatoes

yogurt

muffins

drinking straws

sandwiches

bread

picnic blankets

plates

Point to some blue things on this page!

How many different colors can you see?

What do you like to eat on a picnic?

doughnut

plums

cherries

hard-boiled eggs

cookies

kiwi

bananas

glasses

chips

knives, forks and spoons

sandwiches

pizza

chocolate

grapes

juice

paper napkins

olives

orange

Let's look at colors

 red yellow pink green orange purple blue brown

grey black white gold silver

Can you match the colors to all of these things?

orange carrots

blue fish

yellow sunflower

green leaves

silver badge

purple pansy

grey rhinoceros

red ladybirds

gold crown

brown dog

Which is your favorite color?

Where can you see something silver?

pink ice cream

black cat

white swan

Let's look at shapes

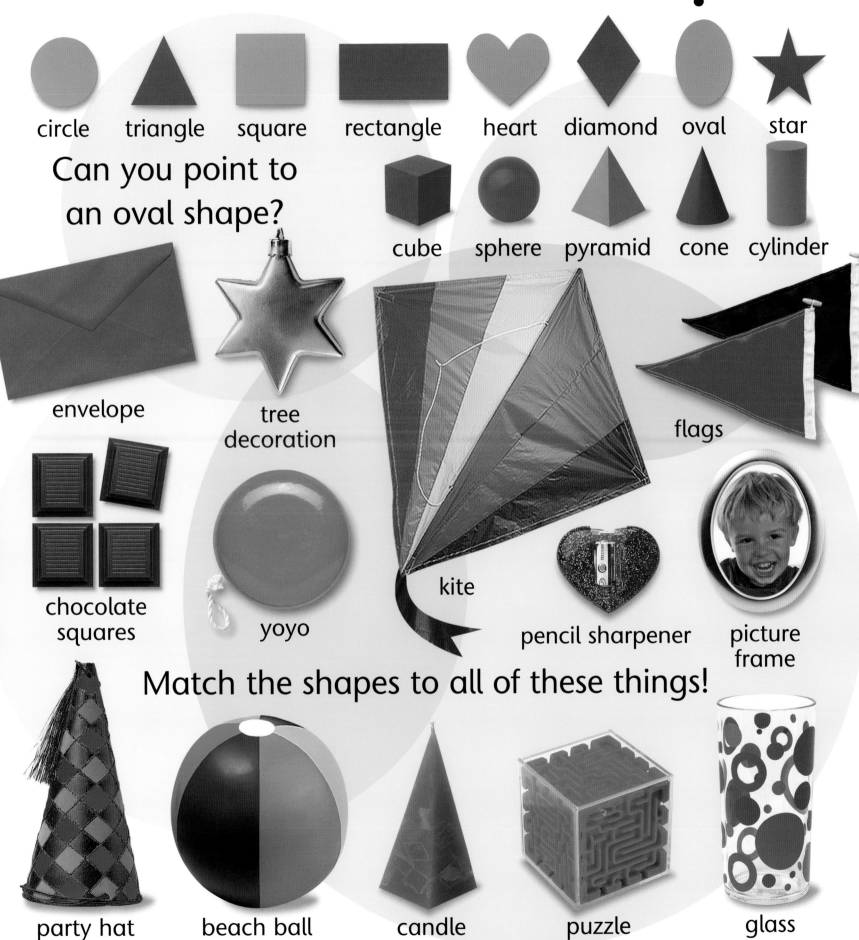

circle   triangle   square   rectangle   heart   diamond   oval   star

Can you point to an oval shape?

cube   sphere   pyramid   cone   cylinder

envelope

tree decoration

flags

chocolate squares

yoyo

kite

pencil sharpener

picture frame

Match the shapes to all of these things!

party hat   beach ball   candle   puzzle   glass

Let's get dressed
Can you name all of these clothes?

undershirt

shirt

T-shirt

underpants

belt

socks

jeans

long sleeved T-shirt

rain boots

sneakers

shoes

tie

Point to the striped clothes!

What patterns are on your clothes?

hat

coat

scarf

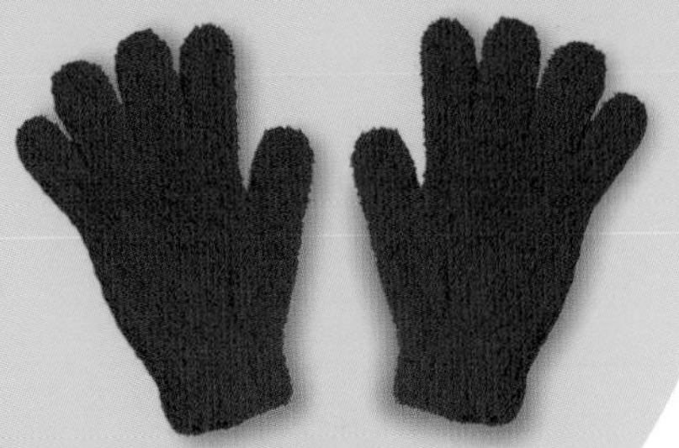

gloves

baseball cap

pajamas

sweater

shorts

Can you match all the patterns to the clothes?

polka dot

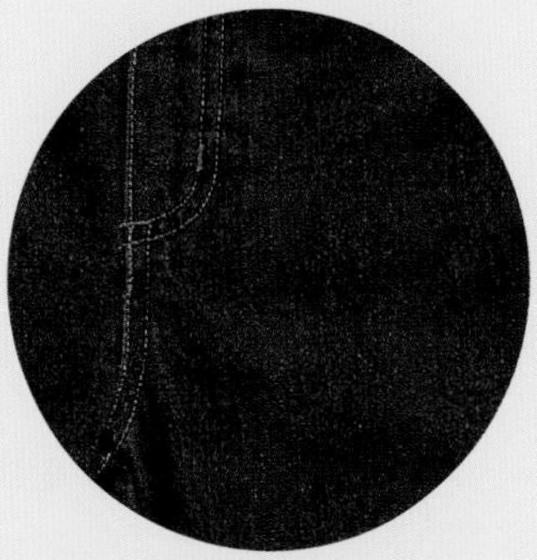

plain

striped

checked

My busy day

dustpan and brush

clothes pins

sweeping

muffin tin

wooden spoons

whisk

I am baking with Grandma.

strainer

apron

mixing bowl

rolling pin

Where are the wooden spoons?

cookie cutters

I am making tea with my friend.

oven mitts

cupcake

What things do you like doing at home?

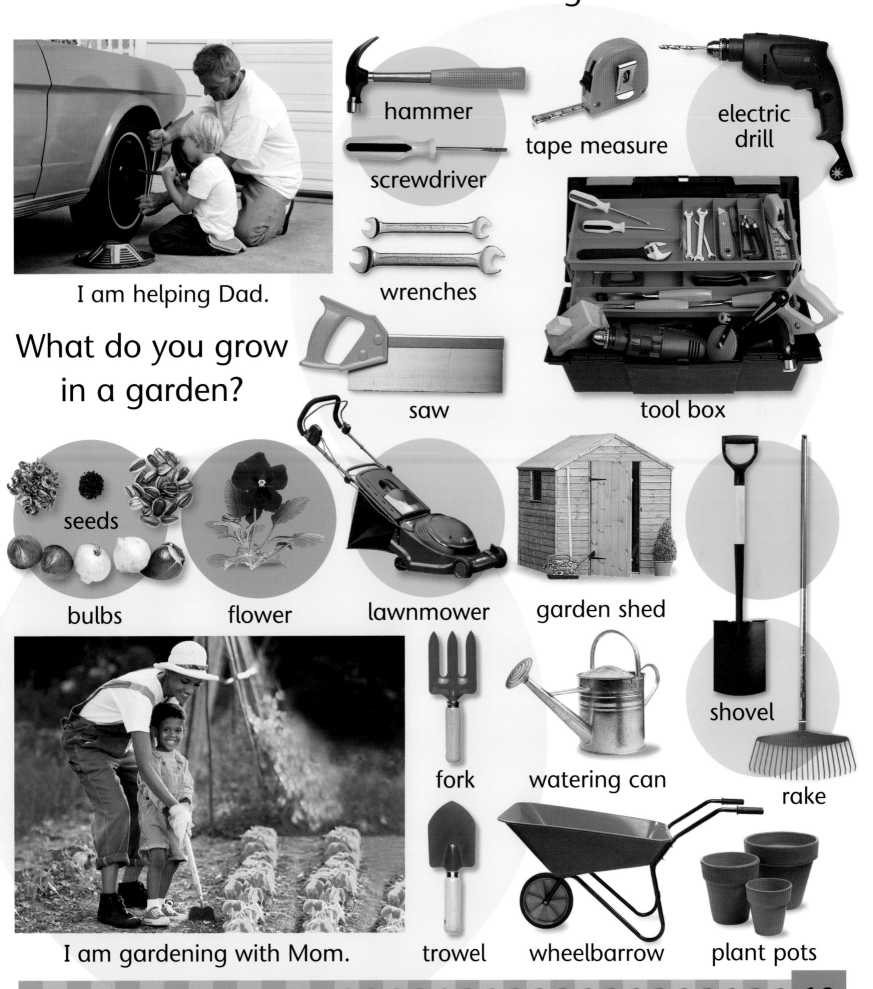

I am helping Dad.

What do you grow in a garden?

hammer

screwdriver

tape measure

electric drill

wrenches

saw

tool box

seeds

bulbs

flower

lawnmower

garden shed

shovel

fork

watering can

rake

I am gardening with Mom.

trowel

wheelbarrow

plant pots

Around the house

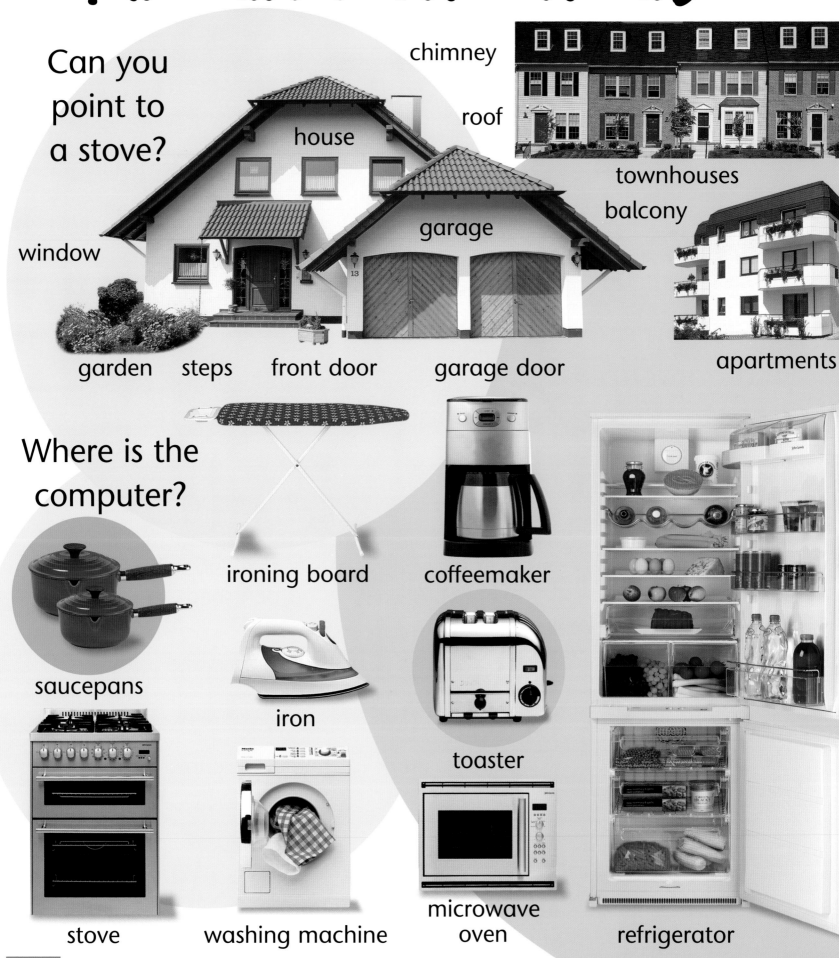

Can you point to a stove?

chimney

house

roof

townhouses

balcony

garage

window

garden   steps   front door   garage door

apartments

Where is the computer?

saucepans

ironing board

coffeemaker

iron

toaster

stove   washing machine   microwave oven   refrigerator

What things can you find in your home?

vase of flowers

table

closet

pillow

vacuum cleaner

shelves

chest of drawers

rug

chair

Where is the clock?

keys

stereo

sofa

armchair

computer

cd and dvd

radio

telephone

television

mug

bowl

knife

fork

spoon

clock

plates

It's playtime!

toy truck

robot

play structure

bat and ball

toy spring

playing soccer

xylophone

dinosaurs

books

drum

tambourine

astronaut

wizard

fireman

pirate

king

Can you point to the boy playing soccer?

backpack

skates

paint box

paintbrushes

playing with
toy animals

Which boy is dressed
as a fireman?

playing cards

modelling clay

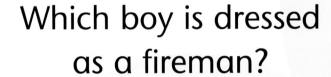
felt-tip pens

scooter

whiteboard

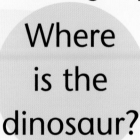
tricycle

Where
is the
dinosaur?

easel

cymbals

guitar

cars

letters

playing an
instrument

marbles

toy blocks

numbers

It's party time!

How many boys are at the birthday party?

balloons

party hats

candies

party blowers

cupcakes

Are there more presents than children?
Are there enough cookies for everyone?
Can every little boy have a party hat?

masks

cookies

milkshake

lollipops

presents

At the beach

How many fish can you see?

water wings

sandcastles

swimming goggles

sea star

sunhat

ice cream

shells

sunscreen

sunglasses

I like listening to the sea in my shell.

I like making sandcastles.

I like digging with my shovel.

Can you find some sunglasses?
Point to some pairs of things!
Match all the words to the pictures!

kite

rubber ring

beach ball

I like fishing.

sandals

swimming shorts

shovel

popsicle

flippers

beach towel

pinwheel

bucket

27

Busy in the bathroom

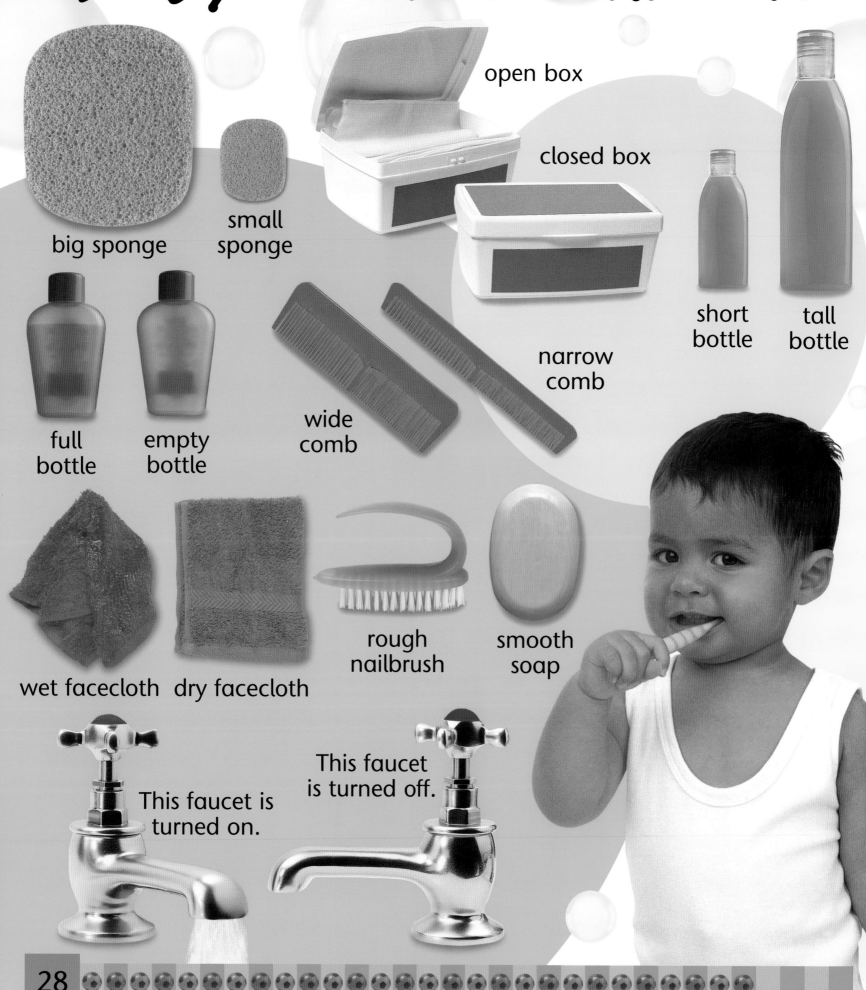

big sponge

small sponge

open box

closed box

short bottle

tall bottle

full bottle

empty bottle

wide comb

narrow comb

wet facecloth   dry facecloth

rough nailbrush

smooth soap

This faucet is turned on.

This faucet is turned off.

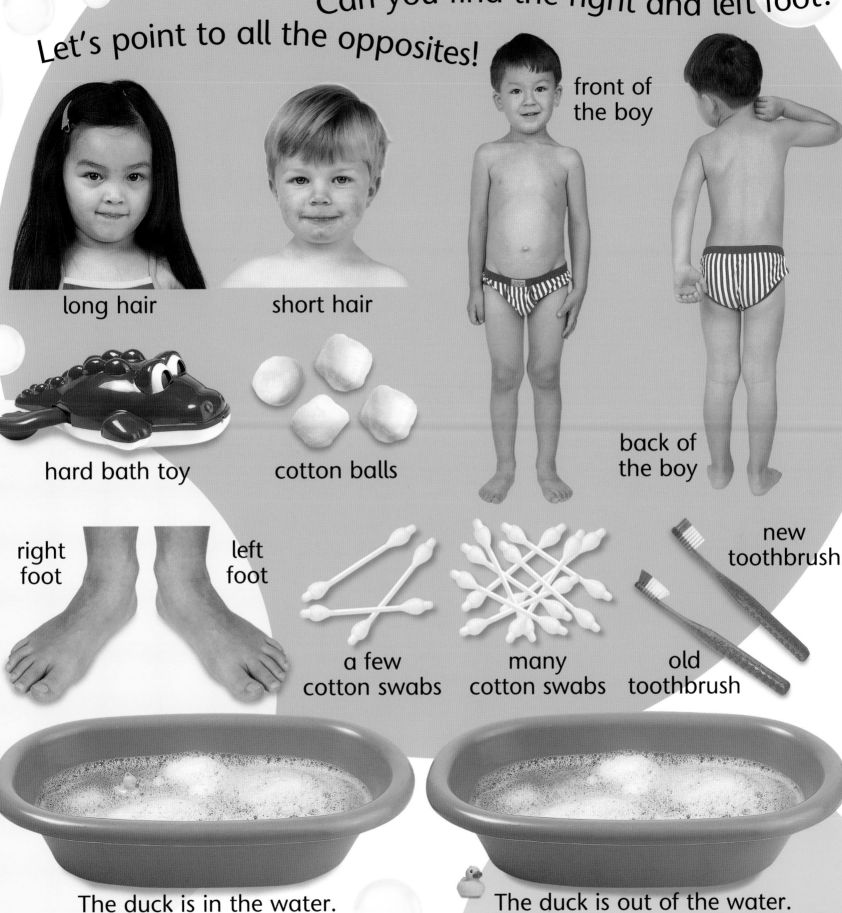

Point to a wide comb and a narrow comb!

Can you find the **right** and **left** foot?

Let's point to all the opposites!

front of the boy

long hair

short hair

hard bath toy

cotton balls

back of the boy

right foot

left foot

new toothbrush

a few cotton swabs

many cotton swabs

old toothbrush

The duck is in the water.

The duck is out of the water.

It's time for bed!

Follow the strings to match the words and pictures!

pillow

moon

I am reading my book.

I am getting undressed

stars

teddy bear

quilt

slippers

Can you help this little boy find his way to bed?
Let's match the bedtime words and pictures!
Can you find all the odd ones out?

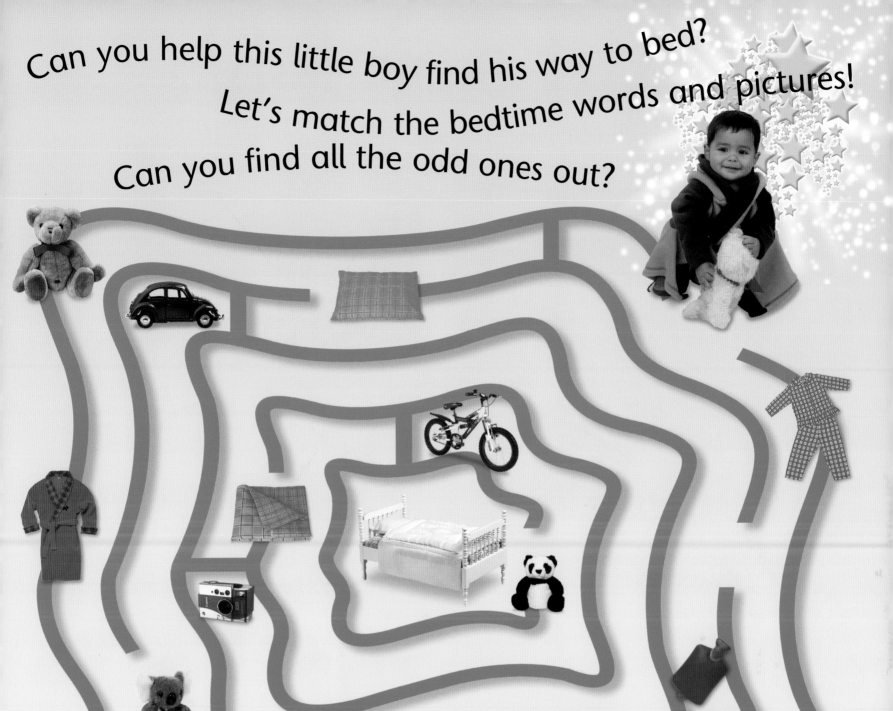

hot water bottle	koala	camera	pajamas	story book	panda
car	snowman	tractor	bicycle	umbrella	lunchbox
pillow	boy	dressing gown	bed	teddy bear	quilt

Let's match!

Where are the robots?   Can you find some jelly beans?

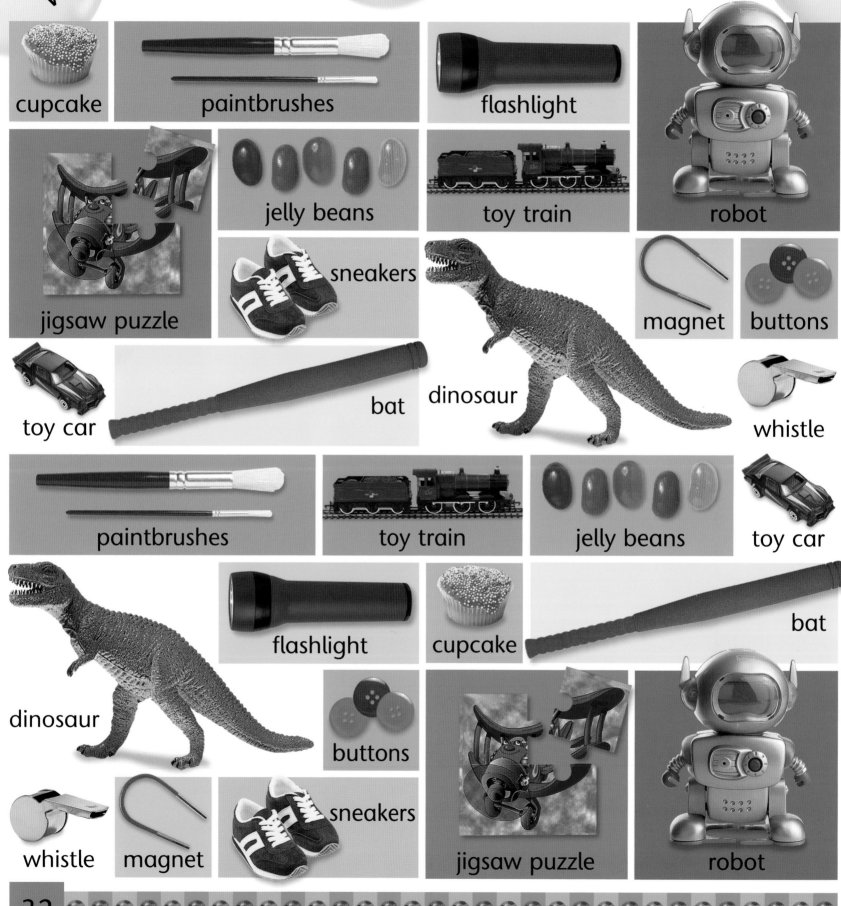

cupcake

paintbrushes

flashlight

robot

jigsaw puzzle

jelly beans

toy train

sneakers

dinosaur

magnet

buttons

toy car

bat

whistle

paintbrushes

toy train

jelly beans

toy car

dinosaur

flashlight

cupcake

bat

buttons

whistle   magnet

sneakers

jigsaw puzzle

robot